BACKPACKER.
Outdoor
Knots

BACKPACKER®

Outdoor
Knots

THE KNOTS YOU NEED
TO KNOW

Clyde Soles

FALCONGUIDES

GUILFORD, CONNECTICUT
HELENA, MONTANA

AN IMPRINT OF GLOBE PEQUOT PRESS

To buy books in quantity for corporate use
or incentives, call **(800) 962–0973**
or e-mail **premiums@GlobePequot.com**.

FALCONGUIDES®

Backpacker is a registered trademark of Cruz Bay Publishing, Inc.

FalconGuides is an imprint of Globe Pequot Press.

Falcon, FalconGuides, and Outfit Your Mind are registered trademarks of Morris
Book Publishing, LLC.

Photos by Clyde Soles unless otherwise noted.
Text design: Sheryl P. Kober
Page layout: Melissa Evarts
Project editor: David Legere

Library of Congress Cataloging-in-Publication Data
Soles, Clyde, 1959-
  Backpacker magazine's outdoor knots : the knots you need to know /
Clyde Soles.
     p. cm. — (Falconguides)
  ISBN 978-0-7627-5651-3
  1. Climbing knots. 2. Outdoor life. I. Backpacker. II. Title.
  GV200.19.K56.S64 2011
  796.52'2—dc22
                         2010034387

Printed in China
10 9 8 7 6 5 4 3 2 1

To the outdoor educators of the world. Though you are underpaid and underappreciated, your work is a true service that can change lives for the better.

Contents

Introduction

Hey, I get it. You're reading this book because you *hate* knots. They're confusing as heck. You don't know when to use the *whosjamacallit* instead of the *thing-amajig* knot. You have no idea what the difference is between a bend and a bight—frankly, you don't care either. Then heaven help you if you ever looked at one of the knot bibles with ten gazillion knots—or a hundred, doesn't matter!

Trust me, been there, done that. When I was growing up, I struggled at pitching tents with twenty-four guylines, often at night and in a storm. Tying down canoes so they wouldn't fly off the rack on the highway was also a challenge. When I first started getting into climbing, I had to learn even more knots that would actually keep me and my partners alive.

At this point, I've probably forgotten more about knots than most people will ever know. That isn't a good thing either, because to this day I still get confused by some knots even though I've tied them countless times. Too much information can indeed be a problem.

When it comes down to it, ropes and knots are functional tools. It's always best to use the right tool for the job. But that doesn't mean you have to carry around an entire hardware store of specialized items when just a few simple tools will suffice. Some tool fanatics might own a dozen specialized hammers, but the average homeowner only needs a basic 16-ounce claw hammer.

The purpose of this book is to give you a tool chest of knots that will cover most applications while remaining portable. We'll leave the obscure specialty knots behind for the aficionados to lug around. Equally important, we'll learn how to wield your tools properly (most effective methods of tying) and which tool (knot) to choose for the job at hand.

Chapter One
Knot Basics

Part of the confusion about knots arises from the terminology. Standing and working, loops and bights, bends and hitches: All have very specific meanings when discussing knots. Alas, those meanings also aren't so intuitive to the average person.

It doesn't matter if a rope is 10 inches, 10 feet, or 10,000 yards long; the part that you are not using is called the *standing part*. What you hold in your hands while actually tying a knot is the *working end*.

When you bend a piece of rope into a U-shape, you form what is called a *bight*. This is the starting point for many knots. If the two strands of the bight cross themselves, then you have created a *loop*, which is also the first step in many knots. Although the difference between a bight and a loop may just sound like semantics, that subtle difference of whether the rope crosses can make a big difference in whether a knot holds.

A bight.

A loop.

If you hang a rope over a bar, you have taken a *turn*—think of it as a bight with a bar in the middle. If you wrap the rope all the way around the bar, you have made a *round turn*. In general, you will take a turn around an object, such as a tree or a tent stake, when you want to adjust the line. And you will make a round turn around a tree or boulder when you want to solidly anchor the rope.

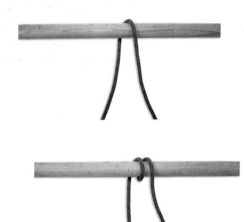

A turn.

A round turn.

Speaking of which, a knot that attaches a line to something is called a *hitch*. You can use a hitch on a post, pile, ring, rail, another rope, or even to the same rope.

Hitch.

When a knot joins two ropes, then it's properly called a *bend*. This term is a little tricky because the exact same form can be called a knot if it joins two ends of the same piece of cord. In practice, the two terms are used interchangeably.

A bend.

KNOT STRENGTH

When people start comparing knots, the subject of strength often arises. This is a mistake. More often than not, the real concern should be knot security—that is, the resistance to coming untied unintentionally.

As someone who has looked at countless tests of knot strength, and conducted quite a few myself, I can assure you that all the charts you see in books and on the Web are deeply flawed. A lot of things that are stated as gospel, such as X-knot holding 60 percent and Y-knot holding 75 percent, are bunk. The truth is that there are so many variables of material and form that such comparisons are virtually meaningless without far more data than most people are willing to digest.

Even climbers, whose lives literally can depend on knots, should not base their knotting choices on "knot strength." The more important considerations are knot security foremost, followed by ease of tying, ease of untying, and perhaps bulk (big knots can sometimes jam in cracks at inopportune moments).

Part of knot security comes from properly *dressing* the knot. This means that you uncross any crossed strands within the knot and snug everything up tight.

In some cases, the knot must also be backed up with an additional knot to prevent accidental untying. For example, when a bowline is used to tie into a climbing harness, it must always be backed up with an overhand knot. Other knots, like the figure-8 loop, do not require a backup because they are naturally secure (but much harder to untie after a fall).

OVERHAND KNOT

A simple and useful stopper knot at the end of a rope that also forms the basis for many intricate knots. As the most fundamental knot, the overhand stands alone as the knot first learned, often by accident, by anyone who handles rope or cordage of any type. A small stopper, it may not meet the demands of all situations. The overhand is repeated time and time again as part of other knots. It can be tied at regular intervals along a line to make the line easier to grip. A tight overhand knot, however, can be very difficult to untie in lines of small diameter and/or wet lines.

1. Create a loop in the working end of a rope or cord.

2. Take the working end over the standing part and back up through the loop. Tighten the knot by pulling simultaneously on the working end and the standing end.

3. This knot reduces the strength of a rope or cordage by as much as 55 percent. Remove unwanted overhands from mid-rope as soon as possible.

Chapter Two
Joining Knots (Bends)

SQUARE KNOT

Also called a *reef knot*, this fundamental joining knot is well suited for binding two pieces of cordage of equal diameter or two ends of the same piece of cordage (as when a package is tied with twine). Remember: right over left, left over right.

This is the knot to use when you want to easily untie the ropes. However, that ease of untying also makes the square knot less secure than other bends. Do not use this for jobs where failure is not an option! It can be backed up by adding more knots to the working ends, but there are better choices.

1. Start with the right rope over the left rope. The right rope wraps under the left hand rope.

2. Now the left rope goes over the right hand rope and wraps under.

3. The result is a perfectly symmetrical knot with both working ends lying next to the standing part.

4. Avoid the granny knot! This happens when you go left and then right over left again. It is far less secure than the square knot.

SHEET BEND

Closely related to the square knot, the sheet bend is one of the oldest known knots, dating back at least 9,000 years. This is a good choice for joining two ropes of different diameter: the greater the difference in rope size, the more secure the knot.

Theoretically, the sheet bend is more secure if both working ends emerge on the same side of the knot. In practice, the difference is minimal, and you should choose a different knot when maximal security is required. One option is to continue wrapping the working end for an extra full turn around the bight to make a *double sheet bend*.

1. Start by making a bight in the larger diameter rope. It doesn't even have to be near an end.

2. Bring the working end of the second rope through the bight, then around the back of the bight and across the top. Then, bring it underneath itself and over the other rope.

3. Pull on each stand of the ropes to secure the knot.

ONE-WAY SQUARE KNOT

Yet another variation of the square knot, this is particularly handy when you need to pull a thicker rope through a constriction with a thinner rope. For example, you can use the one-way square knot after using a light cord for a heaving line and you now want to pull a heavier rope over a limb. Because the working ends point in one direction, they are less likely to snag.

1. Start by tying a square knot with the two ropes.

2. Then take the working end of the narrower cord and wrap it over and then under the standing part.

3. Finish by tucking the working end back through the bight. Notice that you have now tied a figure-8 around a bight of the other rope.

WATER KNOT

When joining two ends of flat webbing, the water knot is a popular choice. It has the advantage of simplicity and reasonably good security. This has long been used by climbers to create loops of webbing that can be untied. I say "reasonably good" because, in some types of webbing, the water knot is prone to loosening when you aren't looking. Sometimes people will stitch or tape the working ends to the standing part but, again, there are better alternatives.

1. Start by tying an overhand knot in one working end of webbing, making sure the webbing is arranged to allow the knot to lie flat if pressed.

2. Now thread the other working end through the knot.

3. Bring this working end around the first knot, essentially tracing it backward.

4. Weave the working end into the overhand knot.

5. When drawn down by pulling hard on all four sections of webbing, the water knot forms a tight ball. Be sure to leave tails at least 3 inches long and work it as snug as possible.

DOUBLE FISHERMAN'S KNOT

Here is the master joining knot for cordage of similar diameter. The double fisherman's is the one to tie whenever you do not want things to come untied. It can be used on thin cord, heavy rope, or webbing. Once this knot has been tightened down, it is extremely difficult to untie!

Also known as the *grapevine knot*, this offers superior security in most situations because the knots tighten and jam against one another when loaded. If less security is required, say for a flashlight lanyard, then a single overhand knot may be used. And when maximal security is required, particularly with slippery rope, then triple overhands can be tied.

1. Start with one working end and tie a double overhand knot by adding an extra wrap around the standing part of the rope.

2. Thread the other working end through the loops of the double overhand.

3. Going the opposite direction of the first knot, tie another double overhand.

4. When snugged up, one working end is above and the other is below the standing parts of the rope.

5. Wrong. If the working ends are both above or below the knot, you need to retie the second half in the other direction.

FLAT OVERHAND BEND

As mentioned, the double fisherman's is the go-to knot for joining two ropes securely. However, that security comes at the price of difficulty in untying. And it is a relatively bulky knot with ends that stick out, so the double fisherman's is prone to jamming when one of the ropes is pulled down a rock face.

For the situation of joining two rappel ropes, climbers have developed the flat overhand bend. This can be used to connect ropes of somewhat different diameter, such as 7mm and 10mm, and can easily hold loads far greater than can be generated during a rappel. The flat overhand is simple to tie and easy to untie afterward. And it is less likely to jam in a crack because the ends point away from the rock as the rope is pulled.

The very simplicity of this knot also frightens people the first time they see it and are about to commit their life to its security. This is how it got the moniker *Euro death knot* (EDK), even though it is well proven in test labs and the field. Some people have been tempted to add an extra wrap, making a flat figure-8 bend, but this in fact is much more dangerous because it tends to roll at much lower forces.

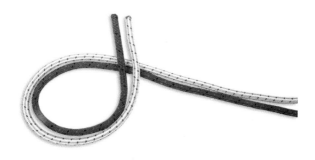

1. Lay the two working ends together and tie an overhand. That's all there is to it. The key point is the knot must be snugged very tightly from both sides. And leave tails at least 9 inches long.

2. When ropes are different diameters, the thinner line should be on the bottom.

3. Finished flat overhand bend.

Chapter Three
Loop Knots

OVERHAND LOOP

The simplest of loop knots, it's also one that creates a lot of frustration. The overhand loop has the unfortunate tendency to practically weld itself into a rope when any part of it is pulled hard. In some cases, it's better just to give up and use a knife to cut off the loop.

1. Make a long bight in the working end of the cord.

2. Bring the working end under to form a loop, then tuck it through the loop to form an overhand knot.

3. If you want to have any hope of untying the knot later, be sure to dress it properly so that there are no crossed strands before tightening.

FIGURE-8 LOOP

Here is the king of loop knots! The figure-8 loop is, of course, just a slight variation of the overhand loop. But that extra turn makes a huge difference both for security and for ease of untying later.

Normally for camping and boating, you will just tie a figure-8 loop as shown here: fast and easy. It can be at the end of the rope or anywhere along it.

1. Start with a long bight of rope and start to tie an overhand loop, only add another wrap.

2. Tuck the working end through the loop.

3. Snug the knot up and try to uncross the strands so that it will be a bit easier to untie.

Climbers routinely use this same knot for tying a rope to their harness. In that situation, you simply tie a figure-8 a few feet from the end of the rope, then thread the working end through the harness and retrace the first knot. There is no need to tie a backup knot for a figure-8 loop, though many climbers do out of fear.

1. The climber's variation of this loop starts with a simple figure-8 in the rope.

2. The working end then goes to the harness, or around an anchor, and back into the knot.

3. Retrace the first knot with the rope.

4. To finish the knot, snug the strand pairs.

SLIP KNOT

The humble slip knot is remarkably versatile. It can be used as a quick-release, a simple noose, a basic pulley, or as a stopper in the end of a rope. Depending on your need, the slip knot can be tied with either the working end or the end forming the loop. Some knotophiles give these two variations different names, but most of us call them both a slip knot.

1. Start by making a loop.

2. Then make a bight and pass it through the loop.

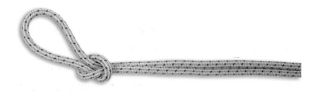

3. Tighten by pulling up on each end and adjust the loop as necessary.

BOWLINE

Seamen have used the bowline for hundreds, if not thousands, of years and it is still considered a primary skill in the sailing world. For decades, climbers used the bowline as the principal knot for tying into a rope, though the figure-8 loop is now preferred by many. Sharp-eyed readers might notice that the bowline and the sheet bend are the exact same knot form, though they are tied and loaded differently.

This is one of those knots that, once you learn how to tie it, becomes a mainstay of your diet—you will go back to it time and again because it is so useful. The primary use for a bowline is anchoring a line to a fixed object; if you just want a loop in the end of a rope, use figure-8 or overhand.

What makes the bowline so useful is the ease of tying once you know the tricks; it can even be tied with one hand. It is moderately secure on its own but can loosen from lots of little tugs. Therefore, in do-or-die situations like climbing, backup knots are required 100 percent of the time.

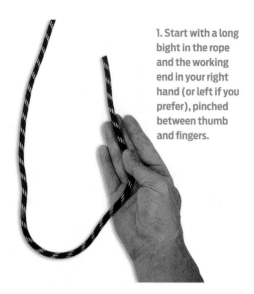

1. Start with a long bight in the rope and the working end in your right hand (or left if you prefer), pinched between thumb and fingers.

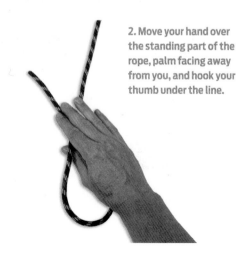

2. Move your hand over the standing part of the rope, palm facing away from you, and hook your thumb under the line.

3. Rotate your wrist so that your palm faces up. This motion creates a loop with the working end already located inside.

4. Now the rabbit goes around the tree and back into its hole.

5. If the rabbit starts from the outside, you get an inside bowline. In laid-construction (three twisted strands), this is more secure due to the way the twists interact. This is the form most people learn and use for all ropes.

6. When the bowline must not untie accidentally, the best method is to add an overhand knot.

7. Finish the bowline, making sure the overhand knot is snugged up tight.

8. If the rabbit starts from the inside, you get an outside bowline. For woven ropes, this is equally as secure and strong. There's no real advantage, but it isn't necessarily wrong with the right rope.

The preceding method of tying a bowline is the one you will likely use most of the time. But here is another technique that is sure to get "wows" from people who have never seen it before.

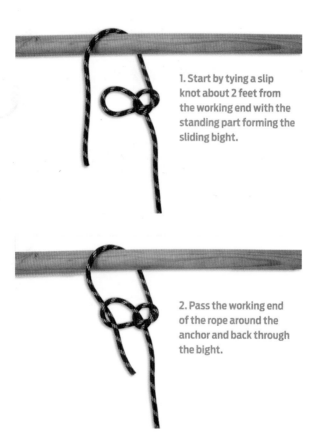

1. Start by tying a slip knot about 2 feet from the working end with the standing part forming the sliding bight.

2. Pass the working end of the rope around the anchor and back through the bight.

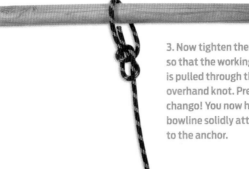

3. Now tighten the bight so that the working end is pulled through the overhand knot. Presto chango! You now have a bowline solidly attached to the anchor.

DOUBLE BOWLINE

Occasionally you may need a bit more security than a standard bowline, but you don't want to tie a backup knot. As with the double sheet bend, you can increase the holding power a bit by adding an extra loop to the working part of the knot.

1. Start by making a loop using the wrist twist but without holding the working end.

2. Now add an extra loop. Then proceed to let the rabbit run.

3. This double bowline provides a bit more gripping power on slippery lines but still should be backed up with an overhand if your life depends on it.

BOWLINE ON A BIGHT

There may be times when you need two loops, instead of one, in the middle of a rope. Climbers use the bowline on a bight to clip two anchor points. This knot can also be used for a makeshift seat (a bosun's chair) if someone needs to be raised or lowered.

1. Start by loosely tying a large overhand loop. The resulting loop should be twice as long as the two loops you desire.

2. Now throw the loop back over the two strands of the rope.

3. Straighten the loop out and rotate the overhand knot.

4. Hold the small loop of the overhand knot with your fingers and draw the two strands of the loop through it. When snugged up, you will have two loops of equal length. If necessary, you can easily adjust them to give you one long and one short loop.

BUTTERFLY

The figure-8 loop is an excellent choice when the direction of pull is directly opposite the loop. Yet when the loop is in the middle of the rope and the strands are pulled apart, it can lock up permanently, and untying becomes a fantasy. For these situations, we use the butterfly knot.

The butterfly is an underappreciated knot that most people and books teach the hard way. Once you learn the simple method, you will find it both useful and easy to remember.

1. Start by making a bight in the rope that is roughly the size of the desired loop. Then give the loop two twists.

2. Flip the tip of the loop backward.

3. Now pass the tip under the two strands and up through the middle hole.

4. Pull the loop up through the hole and snug everything up. The finished butterfly can take load from many directions and still untie with relative ease.

The following alternative method for tying the butterfly does indeed work. But many people find remembering the sequence a difficult task. And the resulting loop is always one size.

1. Start by making three wraps of the rope around your hand.

2. Take the loop closest to your fingertips and move it between the other two turns.

3. Now take the new loop that is closest to your thumb and move it all the way past the other two loops.

4. Stick your thumb between these loops and grab the outer loop you just moved and pull it through.

5. Shape the knot by pulling on the loop and the two main sections of the rope.

6. Tighten the knot by pulling on the two main sections of rope.

INLINE FIGURE-8

There may be times where you have one end of the rope anchored and you need a loop that can be pulled against the anchor. Although the figure-8 and butterfly loops will work, there is a better solution that is also super easy: the inline figure-8.

1. Start by making a bight pointed away from the anchor.

2. Then tie a regular figure-8 loop but only wrap around the line that goes to the anchor.

3. Snug up both the loop and the working end of the rope.

Chapter Four

Attaching Knots (Hitches)

GIRTH HITCH

The fastest way to attach a loop to a tree, pole, or even another loop is with a girth hitch. This simple knot works well when both strands are equally loaded. However, it tends to slip easily when one strand takes most of the load; use a clove hitch instead. Other names include: lark's head and cow hitch.

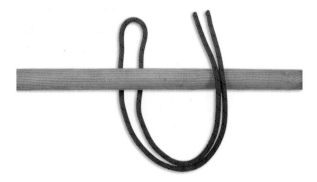

1. Pass the loop around the object and run the working end through the standing end.

2. The girth hitch is strongest when the lines run straight off the anchor point.

The girth hitch is commonly used by climbers for connecting two runners (loops of webbing). This isn't quite as strong as joining them with a locking carabiner, but it is safer than using a single non-locking carabiner.

1. A girth hitch can be used to attach one loop to another.

2. For maximum strength when connecting two loops, flip the loop forward, creating what is sometimes called a strop bend.

3. The final form is identical to a square knot.

CLOVE HITCH

This is one of the most commonly used knots by boaters and climbers. And it is frequently needed for camping as well. The clove hitch is a fast method of attaching a line to an object. Even better, it is easy to adjust and can usually be untied without difficulty after loading. The clove hitch is such an important knotting skill that it is worth your time to learn several methods of tying it.

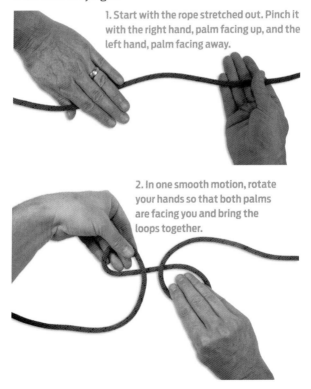

1. Start with the rope stretched out. Pinch it with the right hand, palm facing up, and the left hand, palm facing away.

2. In one smooth motion, rotate your hands so that both palms are facing you and bring the loops together.

3. Once your hands meet, you have a ready-to-use clove hitch.

4. Slip the loops over a pole or tent stake, or clip the loops to a carabiner, then tighten.

1. Another easy method is to grab the rope with your hands crossed.

2. While holding the rope, uncross your hands so the palms face each other.

3. Bring the loops together.

4. The clove hitch is ready to be attached.

Among the most common uses of the clove hitch is anchoring to a carabiner. This is something that behooves you to practice until it's second nature.

1. Start by clipping the rope into the carabiner. Then reach to the line farthest from you and pinch it with your thumb facing down.

2. Rotate your hand so the thumb faces up and bring the rope around the front to the carabiner gate.

3. Adjust the length of the rope as needed, then snug both strands up tight.

Another frequent use for the clove hitch is anchoring to a tree or other fixed object. This can be a fast attachment that is still easy to adjust.

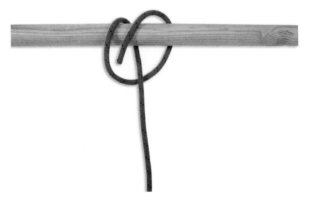

1. Pass the line behind the object. The working end then goes around the standing part of the line. Pass the working end back behind the object and through the bight.

2. Tighten the clove hitch by pulling on the standing part of the line.

TWO HALF HITCHES

Many times it will be difficult to clove hitch directly to something like a tree with lots of branches in the way. In these situations, it may be easier to clove hitch to the rope that goes around the tree. This can also make it easier to adjust the length of the line. For greater security, you can add a full turn of the rope around the anchor point, but this often isn't necessary.

1. Pass the line around the object. The working end then goes around the standing part of the line and out next to the object, creating your first half hitch.

2. The working end continues around the line and back up toward the first half hitch. Sometimes you may want to throw in a third or fourth half hitch for greater security.

3. The two half hitches, a.k.a. a clove hitch, are then tightened against the object by pulling on the working end and standing part.

4. Beware of accidentally tying a girth hitch! This is far less secure and should be avoided.

BUNTLINE HITCH

When you want to anchor a line semi-permanently, you can tie a clove hitch to the line only backward. Called a buntline hitch, this locks the working end tight against the object. Once this knot has tightened, it can be very difficult to remove.

1. Take the working end of the rope around the attachment point and back across and around the standing part.

2. The working end then goes through the loop and in front of the two loop strands.

3. Adjust the length of the line carefully before tightening the knot.

QUICK-RELEASE HITCH

Many times when attaching a line to an anchor point, it is desirable to release the knot quickly. I frequently use this quick-release hitch to tie up boats or to hang food in a tree. The main caveat is the knot requires a lot of spare rope.

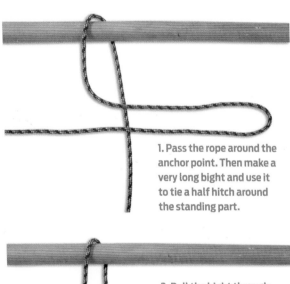

1. Pass the rope around the anchor point. Then make a very long bight and use it to tie a half hitch around the standing part.

2. Pull the bight through and snug this hitch up close to the anchor.

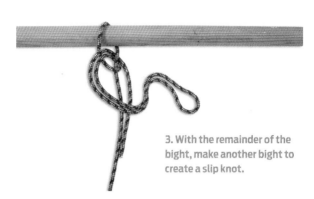

3. With the remainder of the bight, make another bight to create a slip knot.

4. When it's time to go, pull the single loop, then pull the working end.

MOORING HITCH

The mooring hitch is even faster and uses less rope than the quick-release hitch, though it is somewhat less secure. If you leave a long tail, this hitch can be released from a distance . . . just don't trip and untie it accidentally.

1. Pass the line around the anchor point from behind and make a loop with the working end.

2. Pull a bit of the standing part forward through the loop, then insert a bight of the working end.

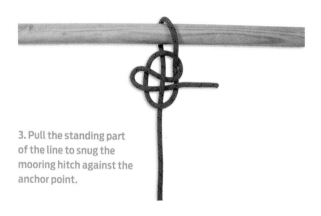

3. Pull the standing part of the line to snug the mooring hitch against the anchor point.

4. When it's time to go, just pull the tail.

SLIP-FREE HITCH

With both the quick-release hitch and the mooring hitch, the line must pass around the object. Sometimes after releasing the knot, the remaining line can catch or wrap around something, preventing your escape. The slip-free hitch solves that problem and is a particularly good choice if your boat is tied up in a swift-moving current.

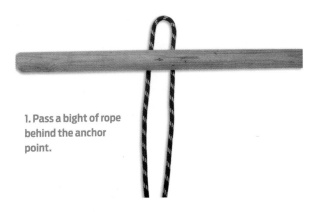

1. Pass a bight of rope behind the anchor point.

2. Bring a bight of rope up from the standing part of line and place it over the first bight.

3. Now make a bight in the working end of the line and slip this through the first bight.

4. Snug everything up by pulling on the standing part of the line. When it's time to go, pull the working end and be ready to shove off in a hurry!

TAUTLINE HITCH

This sliding knot is one of the most common methods for adjusting guylines on tents. The tautline hitch is a variation of a clove hitch with a few extra turns around the standing part of the line for additional grip. The more turns you add, the more grip the hitch offers, though it also becomes harder to slide.

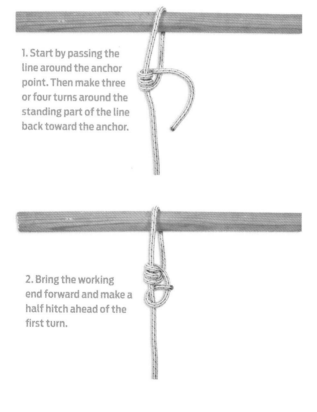

1. Start by passing the line around the anchor point. Then make three or four turns around the standing part of the line back toward the anchor.

2. Bring the working end forward and make a half hitch ahead of the first turn.

3. Be certain that the finished knot resembles a clove hitch. If it looks like a girth hitch, the tautline will not grip as well and may even untie accidentally.

GUYLINE HITCH

This knot is so simple and so effective, you may wonder why people even bother with metal or plastic line tighteners. The guyline hitch can even be backed up with an overhand knot in the working end to prevent it from being loosened too far.

1. Tie two overhand knots about 3 inches apart and roughly 3 or 4 feet from the end. Pass the working end around the tent stake and back through both knots from the front.

2. Shorten the length of the loop by holding the first knot and pulling on the working end. Lengthen the loop by holding the second knot and pulling on the loop from the front.

TIMBER HITCH

This is so simple it's almost not even a knot. But the timber hitch is remarkably effective for dragging logs and lifting heavy poles. The more wraps you add, the greater the holding power.

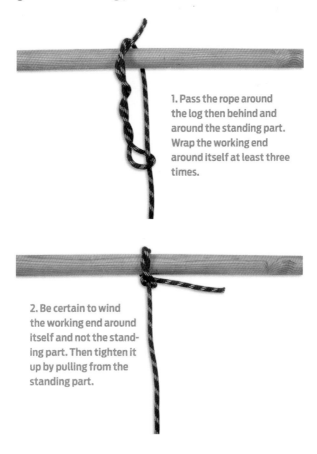

1. Pass the rope around the log then behind and around the standing part. Wrap the working end around itself at least three times.

2. Be certain to wind the working end around itself and not the standing part. Then tighten it up by pulling from the standing part.

3. When dragging logs, you gain directional control by adding a half hitch a foot or two in front of the timber hitch. For the pedantic, this is called a killick hitch.

TRUCKER'S HITCH

In use long before there were trucks, this remains an excellent hitch for cranking tight on a rope. The trucker's hitch gives you a 3-to-1 mechanical advantage like a primitive pulley, so it is excellent for tying canoes onto the roof of a car and pitching large tarps. Note that you should move the slip knots occasionally or the rope-on-rope contact will wear through and break.

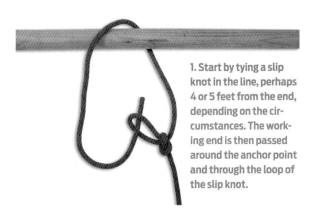

1. Start by tying a slip knot in the line, perhaps 4 or 5 feet from the end, depending on the circumstances. The working end is then passed around the anchor point and through the loop of the slip knot.

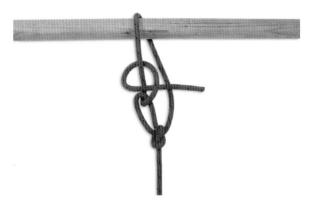

2. Pull tight on the working end and secure with two half hitches or a quick-release hitch.

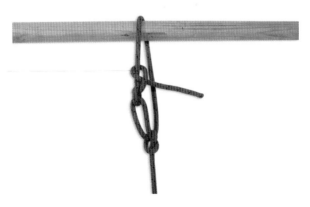

3. You've finished the trucker's hitch.

CLEAT HITCH

There is a proper way to tie off to a cleat on a boat or dock. There are also many wrong ways. Learn the correct method if you will spend any time around waterfronts.

1. Start with a full turn around the base of the cleat.

2. Then bring the working end over the cleat and under the horn before reversing direction.

3. Cross back over the cleat and under the other horn, then go back to the first horn and finish with a half hitch.

4. A properly hitched cleat is neat so that it is fast to untie.

PRUSIK HITCH

Perhaps the best known friction hitch, this knot is used by climbers to ascend a fixed line. The Prusik hitch can also be used for adding a loop anywhere along a line to hang things and easily adjust their position. It can be used as a handle too, but only if you pull on the loop because it slides when you grab the knot.

With the Prusik and the Hedden hitches, they work best if the loop is made of cord that is roughly half the diameter of the rope. Thicker cord may require more wraps to provide adequate friction. And thinner cord has a tendency to lock so tight that the knot is almost permanently fixed to the rope.

1. Pass a bight of the loop around the rope.

2. Add one or two more full wraps.

3. Snug it all up by pulling on the working end of the loop.

HEDDEN HITCH

The Prusik hitch grabs when the loop is pulled from any direction. But it only has moderate grabbing power and can sometimes be difficult to release. If the loop will only be loaded from one direction, the Hedden hitch is a superior alternative. This is the best choice for ascending a line. An inferior version of this hitch is called the klemheist knot; it's essentially the same but upside down and has less holding power.

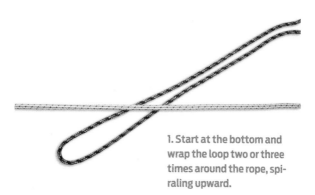

1. Start at the bottom and wrap the loop two or three times around the rope, spiraling upward.

2. Pass the long top bight through the short lower bight.

3. Snug the hitch by pulling on the loop. Release to slide by prying on the lower bight.

MUNTER HITCH

The Munter hitch is used by climbers for belaying a partner. In an emergency, it can also be used for rappelling or lowering a heavy object. The Munter hitch does require the use of a pear-shaped locking carabiner (called an HMS carabiner) to prevent a catastrophic accident.

Some people object that this hitch can cause kinks in the rope. However, this is a case of user-error caused by holding the belay hand off to the side. When used properly with the belay hand parallel to the running rope, there is very little twisting.

1. Start with the rope clipped into the HMS carabiner.

2. Grab the strand farthest away with your palm facing away and thumb downward.

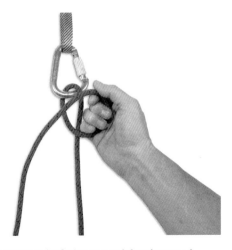

3. Rotate your wrist to palm facing you and thumb upward.

4. Move your hand in front of the other rope and clip the loop into the carabiner. Then lock the gate.

5. The person or object is lowered by carefully allowing the rope to slide through your brake hand. If necessary, you can temporarily tie off the Munter with a quick-release hitch.

Chapter Five

Wrap-Up

There you have it, your new tool chest. A total of thirty knots that are likely to be useful when backpacking and camping, boating, and climbing. Six of these are joining knots, eight are loop knots, and fifteen are attaching knots. If you look carefully, there are really only about a half dozen knot forms that simply get combined in different ways.

Of course there are dozens of other knots that I could have added. But the odds are that you would never use them. Or perhaps you might use a specialty knot once and then forget it. Worse, you might become so overloaded with knot information that you would start to forget the ones you really need. Keep it simple.

The real secret to tying knots is practice, practice, practice. That means physically tying knots but also visually inspecting knots that others have made. I can now tie a bowline with one hand and my eyes closed. I can also spot a mis-tied figure-8 knot on a partner's climbing harness from 30 feet away—many a serious accident could be prevented if all climbers did this. After I've tied my own raft up, it's now a habit to scan the knots mooring other boats so that nobody has to go chasing downstream.

Do yourself a favor and go tie one on!

INDEX

ABOUT THE AUTHOR

Clyde Soles is a professional writer and photographer who has been tying knots for five decades. He is the author or co-author of nine books. Clyde was also the founder of *Trail Runner* magazine and a Senior Editor at *Rock & Ice* magazine, where he wrote numerous gear reviews. To learn more about Clyde, visit his Web site at http://clydesoles.com.